GH00865076

Modern Man-Beast

Vol 1: Roads Less Travelled

Lancelot Chancel

Lancelot Chancel
Tobago Artist & Poet
07948 501 450
Contemporary Caribbean Expressionism

ISBN 978-0-244-69111-0

Modern Man-Beast

Foreword

Men have adapted to many changes in their environment over millennia. Natural disasters and conflicts, migration and technological advancement, have all seen many men transform themselves to ensure their survival; some others have fared less well. Perhaps the greatest challenge to men's adaptive abilities has now crystalized; it gleams brighter than ever before in history. Can men adapt to half of the humans on the planet being drastically different from 30 years ago; 30 months ago; or even 30 days ago?

As women adapt at pace and emerge beyond the ideas that once held them in a place that was not always of their choosing, similarly, men too can adapt beyond old ideas. But I believe to do so in an intuitive way, they must look back and examine from their youth, all the painted parts of themselves, that have come together to create the modern mindset that they now possess. Men must deconstruct that version of themselves, inspecting each component through new eyes. They must then embark on a reconstruction that will, in partnership, create engines that will propel the human species, faster and further forward—and in abundant directions never before fathomed by any gender.

Let us begin the look back, as we endeavour to take a drastic leap forward!

1. Warm Glow

We must not deny, nor ever pretend
Like a nurtured seedling with flower
Pride abounds and sensibilities tower

It is ours alone, to do with what?
Bend it, shake it, make-shift radiator?
Gladiatorial understandings grow greater

Amazement, embarrassment, concern
Replaced by wonder and honour
Hidden from brother, sister, father, mother

Novelty, scary. His if, and her maybe
Growth sectors, spontaneous. Blameless?
Range extended, amber uncontrolled reckless

Demonised, caricatured and idolised
Shifting of mental gear, but always aware
Pulsing, struggling, prying societal stare

Bolted to frame, occasionally aimed
Misdirection, biological communication
Sanctioned instrument of connection

erection.

2. Once

She's looking at me, so differently
So frequently, so something, I don't know
We're having fun, her dimples
Darkened skies, eye corner wrinkles

Laughing with them, looking at me
I take her hand, we dance and stare
Stare and dance, from ear to ear
Giggles and brushes of cheek

She's hugging me differently
Hands on my ribs, breathing deep
I can hear her swallow, tongue against teeth
We taste life, as our wet mouths meet

Repeatedly, repeatedly she's grabbing
I'm touching, she's not stopping me
Are they watching? Do I care? Maybe
Holy Smith! I can feel her heart in my chest

Too many eyes, we're leaving
Who said that? Where are we going?
Lead by the hand, meanderingly more
Too awake to think next, or jinx next

How am I supposed to know?
Breathe slower, move lower
Buttons, zips, hooks, clips
She must think I'm so scrawny

Summer night, garden lights
Din in sight, eyes alight
Once

3. Pins & Needles

The forest, for some the protector of soil
Hugging its surface like warm soldiers crawl
Taming elemental forces it bows at man's touch
Its fate; selection, preservation, never loss.

Laid bare are the lands of so many
Millions of memories where majestic once grew
Purpose and culture caused their end, sadly
Why fear we the forest of these few.

Drizzles of lushness barely mustered
Sporadically dispersed by still-born seed
Adored and equally abhorred but measured
Many masters keen to destroy as weed.

Barren bliss, so seen by many?
What of it? I truly need no shade
See extruded rock and contoured valleys
Welcomed by ponds in which they wade.

The land that we own, our dictator
We merely survive its designed whim
Loving what you're told and your narrator
Serenity. You've only been given one chin.

4. Invisibility

Pearly smiles of perfection
Complexion glowing, infallible
Starlight eyes dazzle and dance
Unblemished silent characters

Aspire you to this?
This Über human creature?
Super models of femininity
Sensual in their perfection?

Denied as childish playthings,
Imagined not perceived
Denied: Horns, Claws and labyrinths of war,
Should we save the queen?

Why condescend? We fight your wars
We fix your tech and lay your floors
The force behind? The belief we're more
You scoff at this?! Disregard our sores?!

Demonstrative desires to protect
To defend the undeserving wretch
Who fall off chairs and garner stares
Nary a thank-you, you may get.

Yes caged to fight, some eyes glow bright
Saviour of scores, not by candlelight!
Not Peter's-Pan, but of iron and of sand
Not boy, nor fan. This trapped, superlative man

Your Sketches

Your Poems

Your Notes

5. Mother warned

Look but don't touch, drink with your eyes but don't taste
Danger awaits, inevitable heartbreak he'll create
Bitterness anticipated, winter precipitation
Deserted and wide awake. Isolated; is this my fate?

Assumptions validated, divergent media propagated
Deep breaths intoxicated pheromones, alive awaken, moisture!
Indeed should not be ventured, no need for sampled tenure;
Silly notion, look away, far beneath me, no time for games

Useless and unequipped, what purpose have I for this
Suffrage? This is not bliss!
Dismiss this nonsense, this lustful mist, domineering madness
But smells oh so good, under spells. Revoke this mood!

I am the he that you probably, always, never wish you could!

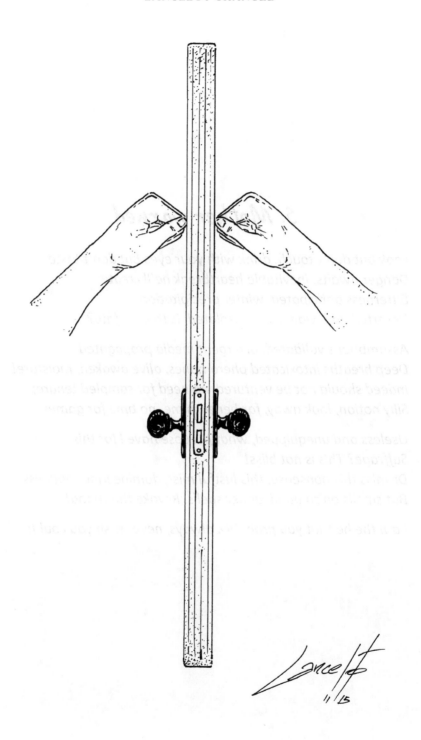

6. Knock kconK

Not my forte to meander. Denial,
Tired river.
Never seeming undecided. On trial,
Judge's splinter.
Left and right oceans crash. Fighting,
Spilt over.
Seeking from others to be. Lightning,
No shoulder.
Lost too far under white water. Stasis,
Not swimming.
Steel Ball turning in glass bowl. Races,
No ending.
Vexed by my echo and rhyme. Predicted,
So obliged.
Perhaps I will exchange myself. Afflicted,
Insignia.

Your Sketches·

Your Poems

Your Notes

7. Shared Territory

Mine alone? Is this whimsical elite myth?
On our dreams of solitude, economies often spit
To each, baring whitened teeth, in daily display
Muscular training weekly, intimate battle foreplay

Walls adorned one day, by hands of masters not seen?
Owning the cave till agreed days? A disembodiment of me
Exchanges of wit and chance, measures of deserving
Observing within exchanges, more brutal is the yearning

Settled subjugation, communal, sedated captivity
Frustrations so normed, we misunderstand life's brevity
Learning together to become what should have been and wasn't
Learning so soft, too slow, distorts the purpose of the lesson

Techniques of self-control must be experienced while thought
To originate and evolve instinct, not listened, nor bought
Noises must be heard, earned ownership truly detonates
From inside it's derived, explosions within must too resonate

The instinctive, displayed and detonated, resonated and educated
Needs no introduction; he stands poised,
Re-masculated from a life; owned.

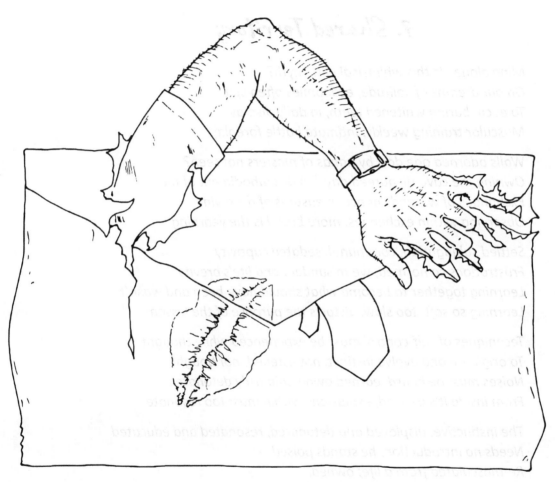

8. The Envelope

It's smooth in here
No one can see inside
Is this you in here, or are you also playing a while?

It's rounded in here
Don't stare at times when it isn't
It's not square in here; no it's nothing like a prison

It's delicate in here
Hold carefully at tummy level
It's numbing in here, mustn't reveal innate decibel

It's narrow in here
Who decided the proper width?
It's shallow in here, suck in, smile, remain stiff

It's shorter in here
Bend lower to accommodate all
Less a quarter in here, such needed to be more of a bore

It's liberated in here
Do use, less of you, please
It's quieter in here; I do declare!

Someone just threw, a new cubicle chair

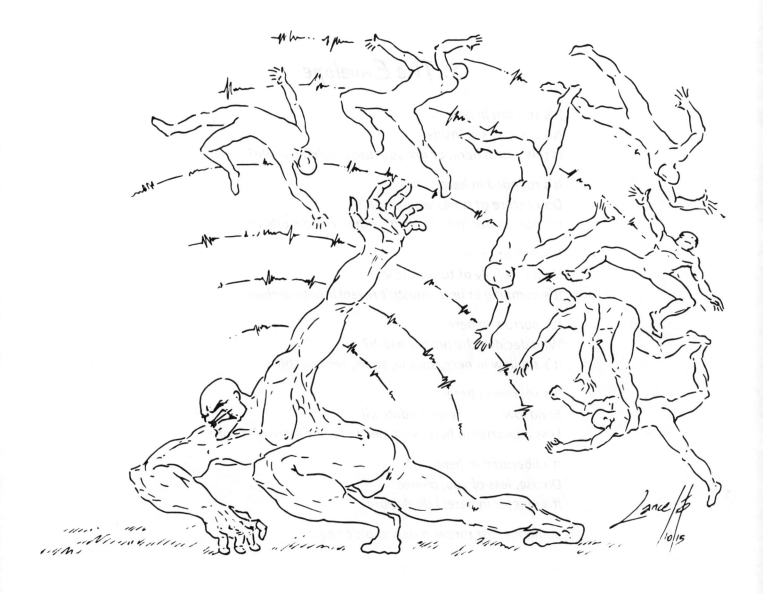

9. No Try

All shall be offered, and all offered again
When there is no more, more shall be found till ruin
This place where we meet is sacred and cherished
It is where motion acts to evidence focus of spirit

The opposite, you hope to be your demise
For only in first stumble do I conjure the demon of theirs
This place where we meet is for the measure of will
It is where your life becomes nothing but the present

Observers are bleating pets to those tasked
Their acceptance; noise, distracting from the air
This place where eyes journey, tongues dry and skin pulls tight
Not fear, carefulness of aim, sensory envelopment drenches like rain

Manipulators of these tools deform human rules
Their brethren in task are held captive and bruised
This place we meet in tribute to body afore mind
You shall never forget these lessons; of effort and instinct entwined

10. Must Be

With wings; how do you Not soar?
With fins; how do you Not swim?
On four legs; how do you Not gallop?
With horns; how do you Not ram?
With voice; how do you Not bellow?

Obligatory or voluntary, life's tethers?

How, does one die?!
How? Not be!
Not be.

11. La mer et vous

I swim because I can
I swim harder because I am
I swim stronger because my destination looms
I swim faster; patience is the virtue of fools

I am burdened; this is my role
I am in training for the future I behold
I am stronger for more burdens do I possess
I am wicked to my body; there is no rest

I have sight of, these fabled shores, for so long did I seek
I have no longer arms, these tools, if only they could speak
I have more in tow now, than when I had begun
I have no need to carry, for the battle's almost won

I saw so many sink in their feeble efforts to swim
I saw so many blink, confronted by rain and these winds
I saw so many examine, this load, this role we share
I saw so many vanish, momentum lost because of fear

I stand the victor on fabled land, battered for a cause
I stand alone and look around and find motive for a pause
I stand atop the corpses of all those that fell away
I stand and they beneath the waves, not far did they stray

Not one dispatched by me but each one bears my mark
Their bodies tethered to my flesh, my burden now so stark
Upon this land, no room for guilt, the past must be no more
Each face I cover within the sand, my mark on most not forged

I swim because I can
I swim harder because I am
I swim stronger because my destination looms
I swim faster; patience was the virtue of fools

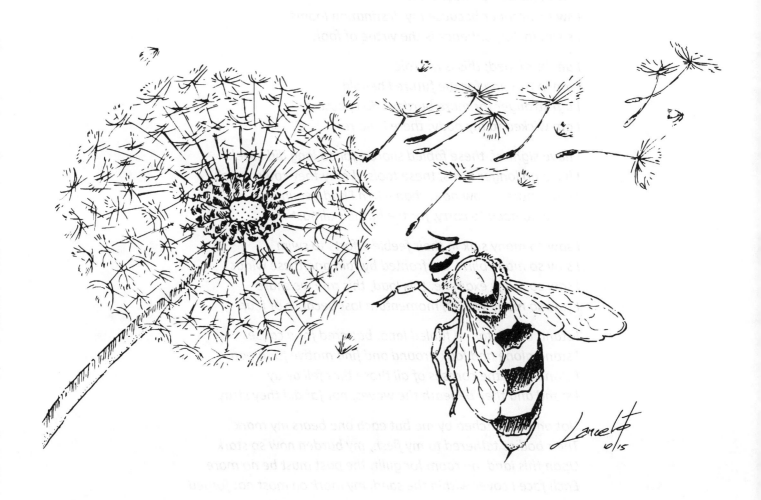

12. Very

Silver skillfully hidden. By darkness,
Shyly smitten. Honest lips forbidden.
To perfection, most singular of selections.
Competition? There is none,
She has already won. My heart,
In safe palms, lightly held. Overwhelmed!

Not toyed with or spoilt,
Never indulged or deprived. Thrives!
Her eyes moist, always misty yet,
Skin sun-kissed, by the city. Alive!
And always with me, Divine!

To hold, truth be told
I don't deserve her; sensual touches;
Inevitably sprouting sonnets.
Banded bees in bonnets, never!
Ever unsettled by the weather,
This intricately simple pleasure; Veronica.

13. Motivations of Man

Competition and the competitor
Possessing and his possessions
Power and its influence
Unity and his union
Freedom!

14. Him, They, The man

I am not the man. Am I the oppressor?
Successor to the throne of deprivation
Architects of ceilings translucent
To nations of those kept subservient?

Do I maintain norms abhorred?
I survive by any means appropriately deemed
Apothecaries needed remedies for bleeding
Hearts torn, ravaged by my fervour, forlorn? Ha!

I've climbed; over all, genders, orientations, colours
I want what is there to be had, by you or by any
Others will stop at nothing. Should I?
My aim is high and fixed only on skylines

Upon that night I do achieve
And wish to see a reflection of me
In the seas around my knees aspiring
Upon the dawn I will recognise, I am

I am him the oppressor, the they
Of which I spoke just yesterday on this hand
Now on the other I stand,
Palm to palm I am,

I am that man

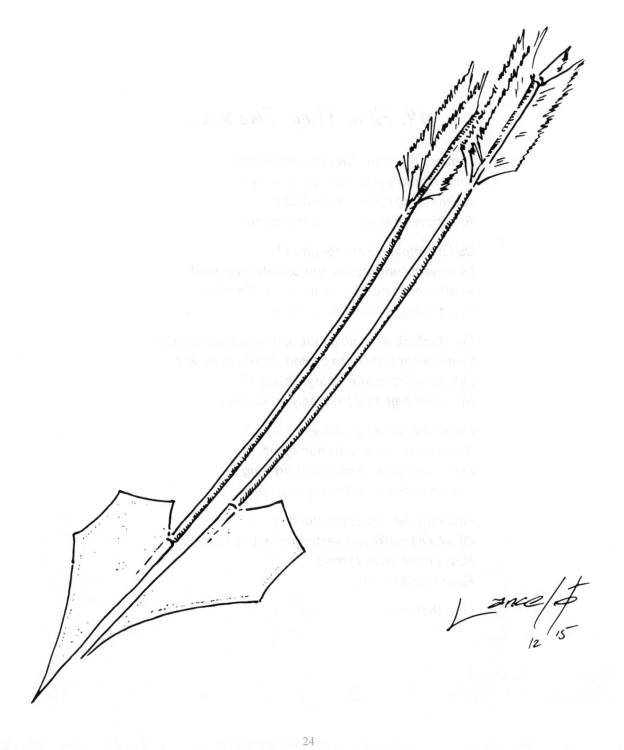

15. Beloved Prey

The hunt-space changes, at times orchestrated
Formations basic, three patterns never changing
Logic shadows instinct, scents intoxicate the brain
The night's selection; occasionally focused on nutrition
Type of hunger satisfied dictate tactics, and position

Choose; those who want to be bitten?
Or those who run the fastest, they that relish competition
Do not; confuse running with fleeing
Those always afraid can never satisfy our rumbling

Never invisible, approaches ghosting and deliberate
Direct to target via methods inconsiderate
The wait out; contemplates the fullest offering
Power introverted while ignorance coyly asserted

Deep breath, the wounded will sometimes fight calm
Subdue desperate spasms with pressured chasms of the warm
Tactility & subtlety, still in tune with proximity
There was no escape, mere illusions aimed to tame thee

The gotten, should be never disappointed
They are the owed, bestowed, evening moan when anointed
Command, though the voyage you may not steer
Relax the weight of desire for the gotten should never fear

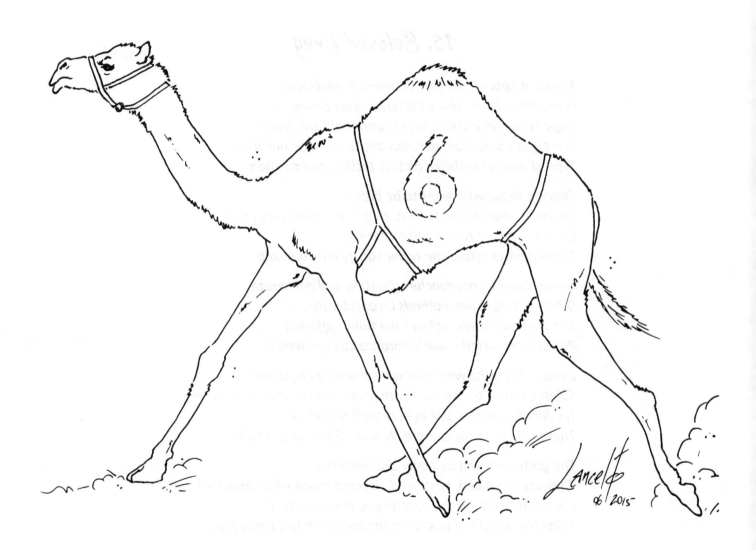

16. Away Games

Why run? Do we fear?
Female, humane, mundane, tear?
Made to run?! Run near.

17. Metro-Gnome

Push the brute, speak him dead
Grunts offend? Remove his head
For we have gained his strength

Must now clap within song
Enters not by his gong
All powers, once held now spent

Soul's embodiment stole
Uncertain of his true role
What of him, you now want?

Softened and not wed
Finessed from toe to head
Pruned. Your hunt he now haunts

18. Different eyes

Glimpse of soft, juxtaposed
Below architectural flow, of torso
Deliberate repose, aglow
Across pupils flow, anticipation

Dimpled tension, inhaled
Fingerprints pale, humidity stale
Outside now, in captivity
Cradled and wrestled, divinity

Perfect, got it, print
You did give a small squint
Finished, clean up, leave
Only denounce yourself please

Your Sketches

Your Poems

Your Notes

19. Blood Donations

Contoured by calluses, and aimed callousness
Sweat and clamour through steam sulphuric
Cut and coaxed, bud bent near broke for Alice's
Bellow, ping and grumble humble, harmonic

Deposit dot, sweep stamp and smear, pigment
Trim form, piercing texture calmly, interlacing
Essences followed, borrowed to indent opulence
Skin lies to eyes, ink spied awry, embracing

Arched, trussed lines toward, adored temples
Ingested emotion, explosions dissolved potion
Warm hold disrobed, moulding repose dimples
Purposed angle, limbs are bramble, spirit motion

Wisdom not owned transposed to those below
Take hold slow and tight, in blackness ripe,
These lands plateau, echo, for those who glow
Arterial souls born of fabric, quilt and stripe

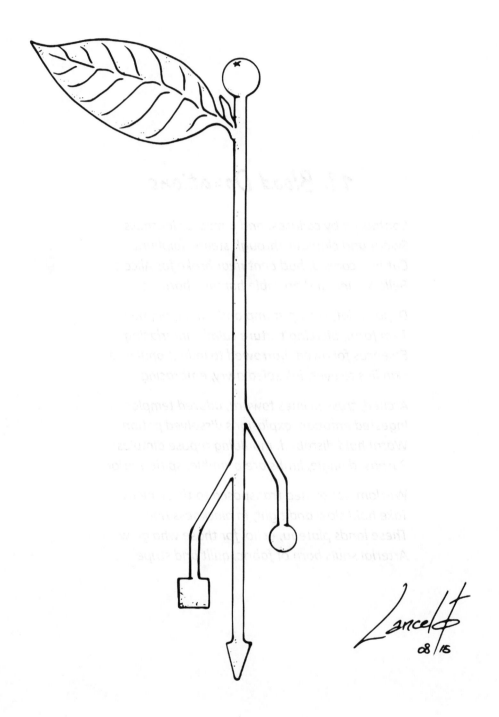

20. Relic

By my brow I eat
It glistens, and my heart is full
By my back I support
Pained, it is warm and a comfort
By my hands I create
So gnarled, a womb it is not

By my legs I carry
Pulsing with purposed blood
By my chest I destroy
Allowing re-birth to flow undeterred
By my feet I tread on ill
Protecting the fruit of my deeds

By my eyes I capture horizons
Unknown but perpetually foretold
By my mind I swim through fear
For the predicted belongs to others
By my lips I ask, now, of soft metal prophets
What of me?

21. Missturbed

Sexual harassment – despicable
Rape – abhorrent
Sexual intimidation & manipulation – vile
Harassment: the continued advancement of proposals
These solicitations for approval – unwanted
Sexual advance: Advance with intent
Romance bent? Hidden content? Microscopic small print?
Stalemate, checkmate jail-traits scent

Intent to acquire and envelop
Intent misspelt, misinterpreted?
Guilt of wanting, thoughts imperfect
Overflowing of want poisoned by influence, power and control
Don't touch. Don't stare. Don't ask. Don't want.
Unless it's ok in that second when it isn't

Secret power in play, no ball games aloud
Invited: limited desire temporarily
Requested: fleeting intent somewhat
Stop! Desire does not mirror dosage advised
Negotiation, proposal, offer, intent
Deflected, redirected, reviewed? To be continued?

Reintroduced intent, content misspelt
Approval denied, despised, reviled
Solicitations, advancements, origination aversion
Ill-preferred sources, selective aggravations
Intent: to acquire, own, envelop, belong to
Adoration perverted, reverted, drowned

No flyers please. Do not harass
Inexperienced negotiators; you need not apply
A lady need only know, that which she does Not currently care to buy.

22. Man; Enough

Suck the stand firm, stay strong bull-trip
I'm exhausted by these pretences, patriarchal and archaic

Atlas I'm not, nor do I aspire to martyrdom, or farces passed off as hard
Human! Bleeding soul and feeling many things, alone I am

Not cold but electrified by the spectrum,
Not excluding the occasional erection, of beacons

To passionate purpose and aggressive pursuance with direction
Unashamedly, this is me. Honestly. Not supposed to be.

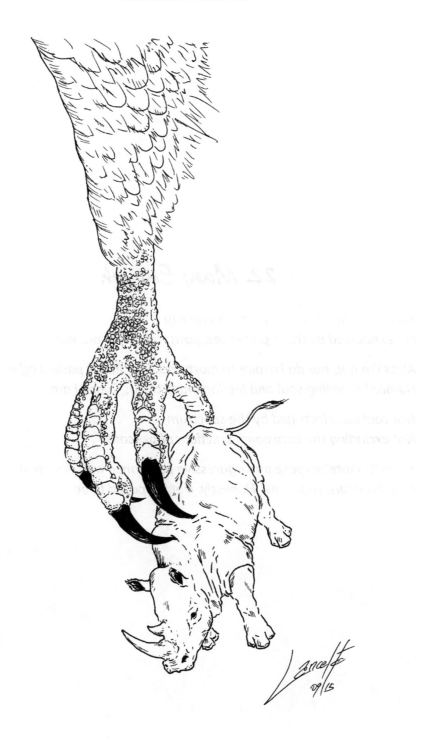

23. Preso

Make no mistake - I want to own and use your body for my elevation
And have your mind held in tune to my purposes for you
I desire your flesh beneath me and your hair in arms reach
I shall perch on your shoulders to hunt the world that you deign to

The smell of you must be smeared on my possessions, as I possess you
I require the sweat of your brow to be for our deliverance
I watch you move like the cat, strategic, tempered, focused and effective
This streamlined machine your body gleams, beautiful to behold and operate

I will touch you and enjoy you, desired pleasures merge with discomfort
Your welcoming caress and beating heart, my lullaby
You will be pleased to belong to me, and by the care that I shall take
Tonight I shall explore your very breath, blink and impulse

Tonight your instructions shall be simple and slowly spoken
Begin with warmth, continue with purity
Tonight you shall bathe and soothe my feet,
For I shall; make you my husband

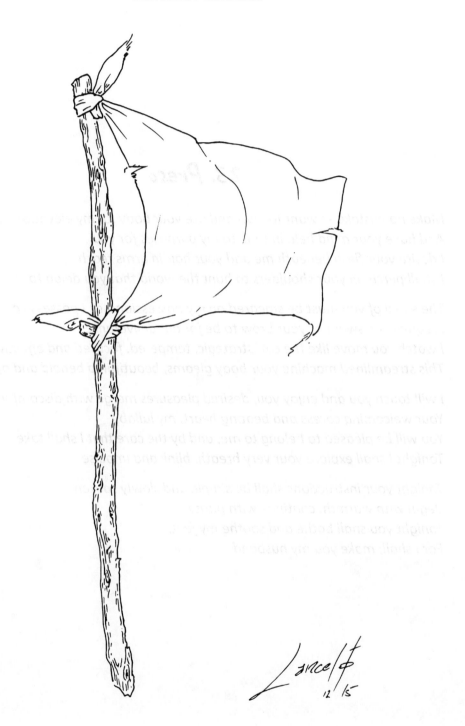

24. Disarmed

Ventures at end, wandering put away
Welcome unseen sores, soothed in warmer seas
Wounds washed, sweetened, by hands that never stray
Swayed to peace hypnotised, so comfortably teased

Shoulders relaxed, undone, palms pale unclenched
Taken and shown, a new world, away due
Warm huddled thoughts, my soul aglow sundrenched
Vigour to be more, restores perfect view

No less the strong, to see spear lay down
Duties of union, and mentor at fore
Taken in hand, in defence of her crown
Not yet imparted, I, besotted to its law

Stand we, now one with audience in tear
Blessings are asked and offered for all time
Ventures anew in wonder without care
Willing beast before thee, intimate, sublime.

25. First Fragment

This isolated encapsulation of my essence
Its mere presence a token of transcendence
Journeys to be mapped, no desire to go back
Footsteps in time luminescent

My yearning to protect, shadowed; carnivorous
To defend through experience from unseen among us
My own tone bestowed on coat bristle grown
Morn' dew, on pupil I stand so oblivious

Guilt upon pride to utter that it's mine
For selfishness I find with a tear in my eye
Thoughts of storing in a box, all covered with locks
Too precious this find, to be deprived

The freedom to exist like a balloon adrift
Confines, all are mist, imaginary and pointless
It sees only now, and as such not soon bow
To the world which corrupts with a kiss

Who would it be, of air, land or sea
Of me, or more of you? Alone or one of two?
It matters not you see for it exists here, today
And now, is able to say, no, up and tree

What it chooses; It will be; My child.

26. Glass Half Empty

I don't understand how to stop
Loving what was much more
Or understand my emotional soup
Brewed by those moments so sour
There are two sides to any story
But my story must now be stored?
All seek to unearth her sadness
Yet I must try to reveal more?

Half of me has been ripped away
I'm over exposed and I bleed
The world says I should be a wall
My heart's comfort isn't a need.
Do they take me out for sunshine?
Who wakes me up at dawn?
Who pops down the shops for me?
Do they ask if I'm settled or warm?

Would they even listen to my truth?
How much I, was hurt on that day
That fights take two to continue on
That I was never the one to stray
But I've had a part in this end
I have hurt others and been hurt more
I have fought taut venomous battles
And we've each tallied our own score

Alas, I am not the victor
The victor is now this void
That consumes and shadows each day
As our conflict did with noise
But I'm droning on about nothing

My old burdens aren't what you seek
But I always appreciate you listening
...So; the same time again next week?

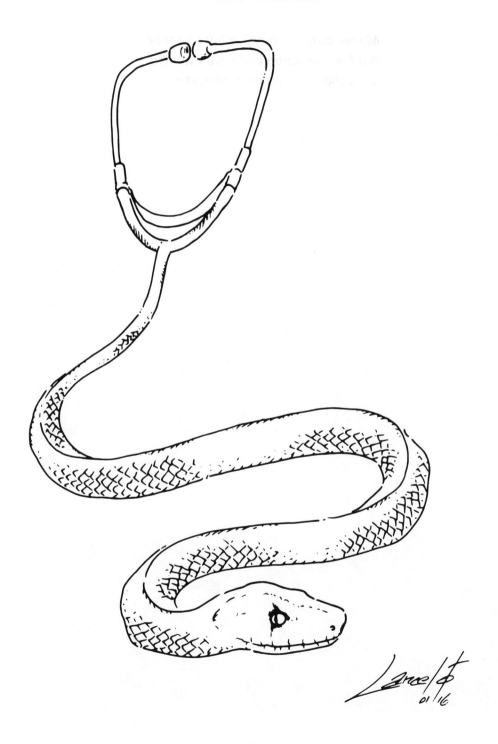

27. General Practice

Always brave, Always fast,
But a sprain means I'm limping in last.
Always prompt, Always alert,
But the cold makes my knees hurt.
Always perfect, Always whole,
But I've found a really odd mole.
Always strong, Always firm,
But dairy makes my tummy turn.
Always immune, Always safe,
But morning rises - two hours late.
Always dependable, and enduring,
But the cut grass keeps me sneezing.
Always focused, Always in tune,
But migraines keep bringing me to ruin.
Always resilient, Always on top,
But half a mile and ankles plead to stop.
Always ravenous, Always engorged,
But shortened breath hints less; not more.

Always I avoid, I ignore and I turn away,
But caring for the details bring peace every day.

Irregularity should be explained
And swelling always seen.
You will have, just You to blame.
Stop pretending that you've already been.

Your Sketches

Your Poems

Your Notes

46

28. Speak now, or forever

The secrets kept to protect me?
The distance created to shield?
The ways you justified silence,
Scale-leaves of onions unpeeled,

Revealing may seem unnatural,
Relaxed chat may diminish esteem,
But if your ideas are never on offer,
Your presence will seem a dream,

Who told you that it's not done?
Who told you words aren't a need?
Why accept old rules made for you?
Escape! For both our lives I plead.

Say what you know even if I know
Say what you feel when you feel
Say how it ended and how it began
Say all the nothingness in between

For if, you fail to show and tell,
And fail to think aloud,
And fail to recite, or remember times,
And fail to draw small crowds,

You exist only in reminiscence,
Time will tame your echoed voice,
Distance blurs your vigorous gestures,
Emotions dilute what was, your choice,

What's more is that we are the poorer,
Seldom offered, thus less we receive,
Speak now; as we're quietly seated,
Speak often, as wind rustles leaves.

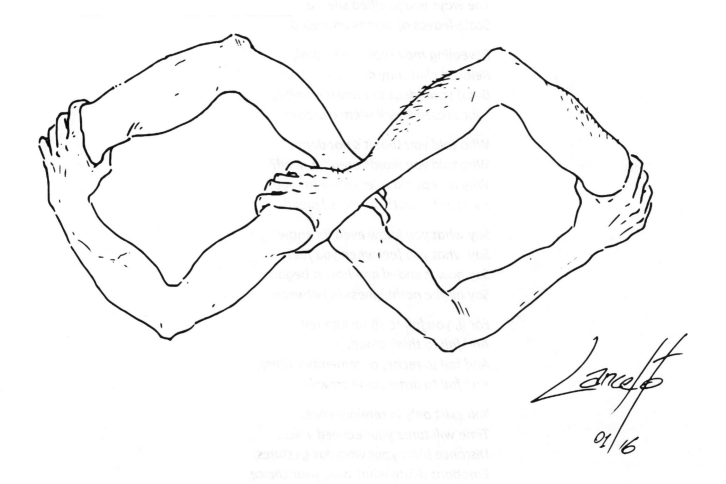

29. Never Ending

Up is down and light is dark
Smiles are jeers, and laughter barks
Aloft are ghosts, less, least and worst
Thorns in legs, arms weakened, eyes cursed

Gone I must be, free from this pain
Catalyst of destruction, I have caused this rain
Erased, Invisible, Removed, Sunken and swirling
Hollow and torn. My only wish? To be burning

Craggy looping pattern, thought tangled in chains
Sees no clear footpath, only cliffs and no plains,
Sees only hurricanes, no kissed breezes and no dew
Sees the above and the below; black and white with no hues

Sees what he sees, as what he sees, sees him,
No desire for new eyes to see beyond this murky sin
Speak he must, of all those penultimate visions
Oblivious to the fall. Amnesia. Vision splintered

Cursed, shattered sight will rarely discover a way
We must extend our arms, pulling from edge to which he strays
Understand, now lost, you are tormented
Understand, now infected, you are blind
Allow yourself to be rescued son
Allow others to be kind

30. Use less Kings?

Every inch of this body
Every path of this mind
Finely tuned to this duty
Further tasks I need not find

Celebrated for my victories
Celebrated by my foes
Stark changes to this landscape
Stark changes bringing woes

The tide has risen further
I have not yet learned to swim
Water warriors invade the border
Casting asunder all rules, all wins

Earthquakes destroy my balance
Removing me from my throne
If I am no longer Provider
Which kingdom, do I call home?

Returning to my beloved people
My head heavy, hung so low
My victories all but forgotten
Hands empty, nothing to show

But I must trust my people
I was chosen by them to stand
Though then and now I falter
Together, with me, they band

They have been learning to swim
They have sought stable earth
They have lifted my head to see
Love not strength defines my worth

Finely tuned to past duties
I underestimated these hands
Every vision of mind refocused
We will find victories upon new lands

###

Thank you for reading Modern Man-Beast – Vol I: Roads Less Travelled.
If you enjoyed it, do take a moment to leave me a review at your favourite retailer.

Follow me on Twitter and Instagram @LancelotChancel